Ethelfleda: the Lady of the Mercians

HEROES AND SAINTS

R. J. UNSTEAD

ILLUSTRATED BY JOHN MACKAY

A. & C. BLACK LTD
LONDON

MEN AND WOMEN IN HISTORY

1. HEROES AND SAINTS
2. PRINCES AND REBELS
3. DISCOVERERS AND ADVENTURERS
4. GREAT LEADERS

Also by R. J. Unstead

LOOKING AT HISTORY

PEOPLE IN HISTORY

LOOKING AT ANCIENT HISTORY

ENGLAND

TRAVEL BY ROAD

A HISTORY OF HOUSES

MONASTERIES

© 1964 A. & C. BLACK LTD
4, 5 & 6 SOHO SQUARE   LONDON W.1

MADE AND PRINTED IN GREAT BRITAIN BY
MORRISON AND GIBB LTD, LONDON AND EDINBURGH

CONTENTS

Pytheas

THE GREEK SEA-CAPTAIN

THERE was bustle and excitement down at the waterside of the port of Massilia. A pile of stores stood on the wharf. Slaves carried jars of wine, baskets of figs and live chickens, bundles of cloth, rope, hides and tools up a plank on to the deck of a stout merchant ship.

Seamen stowed the cargo in the hold while their captain gave orders to the men who were testing the rigging and shaking out the great sail.

A passer-by joined the crowd of citizens on the quay:

"Why is everyone watching a ship being loaded?"
he asked.

"You must have been sleeping, friend," answered
his neighbour, "if you do not know that the Council
of Six has chosen Pytheas to sail to the north in
search of tin."

"Pytheas the navigator?"

"That's the man, the bravest and most cunning of
all our captains."

"But what of those cut-throats, the Carthaginians?
Will they not sink his ship before it even reaches the
Pillars of Hercules?"

"Friend, you must be deaf as well as stupid.
Surely you know that Carthage has made war on
the city of Syracuse? The fleet of Carthage has sailed
to other waters and the way to the unknown Ocean
is open."

The citizens of Massilia were Greeks who had
made their home in what is now called the South of
France. They traded along the shores of the Mediterranean Sea and they also went inland to do
business with the Gauls who liked to buy the beautiful and useful goods which the Greek merchants
could supply.

These Greek traders were afraid of the Carthaginians. Carthage was a splendid town on the north
coast of Africa and, at this time, the Carthaginians
were the best sailors in the world. They sailed through
the Straits of Gibraltar, known as the Pillars of

Hercules, and brought back cargoes of tin and amber from the unknown lands of the north. They would not let any other ships pass the Pillars, so no one knew where these precious things came from.

But now the Carthaginians were at war and the Council of Massilia had decided to send a ship to discover the mysterious Tin Islands.

They chose Pytheas to be captain because he was not only brave but he was also a clever seaman who could read the stars and measure the distance of each day's sailing.

At last the ship was ready. Prayers were said and sacrifices were made to the Goddess Artemis who watched over the city. Then the graceful ship moved out to sea. Pytheas ordered the steersman to keep the bow pointing to the west.

First, the ship sailed along the coast of Spain and through the Pillars of Hercules. The sailors could see the African shore, but there was no sign of Carthaginian warships. Presently, they came out into the great ocean and turned north.

The sea was rough but the little ship rode lightly over the waves. By day, Pytheas kept within sight of the shore, for he knew that his sailors would be frightened if they could not see land. At night, they lowered the sail and rode at anchor in some quiet bay.

As they sailed northwards, the sky became cloudy and sometimes the sea was covered with a cold mist that the Greeks had never known before. But Pytheas told his men not to be afraid. They must be near the Tin Islands.

    *   *   *   *   *   *

A year passed and then another. Sometimes, in the market-place of Massilia or in one of the wine-shops along the water-front, men would talk about Pytheas and shake their heads:

"He must have offended the goddess," they said. "Perhaps he has been wrecked or eaten by the giants that dwell in the North."

One evening, a ship came slowly into the harbour of Massilia. Its sail was stained and patched, its planks were weather-beaten, but its ragged crew waved and shouted like men filled with a great joy. People ran to the harbour and the sailors' cries reached them across the water:

"Pytheas! Pytheas!" they shouted. "Pytheas has come home!"

The elders of the city hurried to welcome their bearded captain. When he had been bathed by slaves and dressed in a new tunic, a feast was held in his honour and, afterwards, while his sailors were boasting over their wine, he told the tale of his great voyage.

"The waters of the Ocean," he said, "are far steeper than those of our own sea. Often we feared for our lives as the waves rose higher than the mast and we were sunk in a valley of green water. But our

Pytheas tells his story at the feast

ship rose like a sea-bird and at last we came to the land of the Brythons."

"Tell us," said his listeners, "what kind of people they are."

"They are like the Gauls," he replied. "They plough the land and grow wheat and barley on the hillsides, but the valleys are filled with great forests and marshes. Yet the people are not savages. Though they live in little houses made of wood, they weave cloth and they have tools of iron and ornaments of gold. They have war chariots but I saw no fighting, for they seem to be a simple kind of people not given to war. In some places, there are great stones set upright in circles, in honour of their gods."

"What of their food, Pytheas? Do they eat like us and drink wine?"

"No, friend, they have no wine. It is too cold for grapes to grow. Instead, they make a drink from barley and honey. We did not like it, for it tastes bitter.

"Nor do they thresh wheat out of doors as we do. Because of the rain that falls nearly every day, they thresh it in big barns. Then they store the corn in pits dug in the ground. As I went further north, I saw that wheat will not grow in such a cold land, so the people live by hunting and by keeping animals for their flesh and milk."

"But what of the tin you went to seek?"

"They take the tin from deep holes, creeping into

Crossing to Ictis with waggon-loads of tin

tunnels cut in the rock. They smelt the tin and hammer it into pieces shaped like knuckle-bones which they carry to an island named Ictis. They wait until the tide has drained the water between this island and the mainland and then they drive waggon-loads of tin across the sand. They say that merchants come from Gaul to buy the tin, but I think that these are Carthaginians."

Pytheas went on to tell how he sailed right round the Tin Islands which were shaped like a triangle. Afterwards, he sailed northwards for six days to find the Land of Amber where the beautiful stones could be picked up upon the seashore.

He came to a country that he called Thule, which may have been Norway, but the weather was so cold that the Greek sailors were unhappy and he had to turn southwards. But he had seen the midnight sun, had learned that the sea sometimes turned solid in the winter and he had noted that as the moon changed, so the tides changed too.

All these strange tales made people wonder if Pytheas was telling the truth. Some said that he was a liar. Others said that his wits had been taken away by the demons of the mist. No one could be sure that there really were any lands beyond the Pillars of Hercules.

Pytheas smiled. He knew that he had spoken the truth. One day, others would sail the same ocean and discover the same islands that he had seen. He had reached Britain, had gone ashore to explore parts of Cornwall and Kent, had sailed into the North Sea and had come safely home with a cargo of tin, hides and amber.

Even if some people did not believe him, he told one of his slaves to write down the story of his great voyage. When it was finished, the Greek slave looked up from his writing-tablet and said:

"Master, what shall be the title of your book?"

Pytheas looked out across the bay and answered:

"I am a sailor. My life has been with ships and all my knowledge is of the sea. Let my book be called *About the Ocean*."

The Britons speak to Caesar

Julius Caesar

A YOUNG officer entered the general's tent and saluted:

"The men from Britain are here, O Caesar," he said.

"Send them in," replied Julius Caesar.

The great man rose and welcomed the Britons, inviting them to be seated, while orderlies brought food and wine. Presently he began to question the visitors: how big was their island? How many tribes were there? Had they any harbours? Was the harvest good?

The Britons answered carefully.

"We are come, O General," they said, "to offer corn and gold. We know how great is the power of Rome and we ask peace for our island. More we cannot say."

Seeing that he could learn little from these messengers, Caesar told them that they could go home.

"I promise you peace," he said. "My friend Commius, the Gaul, will travel with you. He understands your language and when I hear from him, I myself may visit your island."

But, as soon as the Britons had gone, Caesar sent for Labienus, his most trusted officer:

"Make ready the ships and the legions, Labienus," he said. "We will sail to Britain as soon as the wind changes. These Britons pretend to be friends of Rome, but for many years they have given aid to the rebellious Gauls. We must teach them a lesson. What is more, I believe that the islands are rich in tin, gold and corn."

Julius Caesar had been commanding the Roman army in Gaul for more than three years. He was now about forty-five, rather bald, with a sharp expression and bright eyes. He led his soldiers so well that they always obeyed him, for although he was very strict, he was fair and he knew most of the men by their names.

On the march, Caesar led his troops on foot. Sometimes, he would dash off shouting, "Follow me!" and they would have to follow for miles over rough country. Sometimes, he would raise the alarm in the middle of the night and order them to march at once. He did these things to train his men to obey at all times, but he would also joke with them and let them enjoy themselves after they had won a victory.

When the fleet was ready, Caesar set sail for Britain at midnight. His force was not very big but every man was well used to hardships and fighting. By morning, the Roman ships were close to the coast of Britain. The soldiers could see high cliffs, with waves dashing against the rocks.

The army could not land there. Caesar gave the order to sail along the coast until he came to a place where a pebble beach sloped down to the sea.

From the cliffs, the Britons had watched every move. They knew that these long ships had not come on a peaceful visit and they were ready to defend their island. The warriors followed along the cliffs and, as the Roman ships came close inshore, they dashed down to the beach, hurling their javelins and driving their chariots to the water's edge.

The Romans were dismayed. Although their archers and sling-men let fly from the decks, the soldiers did not move. They were afraid to jump down into the waves. The shore was lined with yelling, painted savages, some of whom were already in the shallow water, waving their spears and daring the Romans to come on.

At this moment, the soldier who carried the Eagle of the 10th Brigade, cried out:

"Jump, lads, unless you want to lose your Eagle. I mean to do my duty. Follow me!"

M.W.1—2

Holding aloft the pole that carried the silver eagle, he jumped down into the water and the soldiers, knowing that it was a terrible disgrace to lose their Standard, leapt after him with hoarse shouts. Men from the other ships followed their example and a furious battle took place in the shallow water and all along the shore.

Gradually, the Romans got a footing on the beach. Then they formed into ranks, charged the enemy and drove them into the woods. They could not chase them any further because the ships carrying the cavalry had not arrived, so they built a strong camp and waited for the morning.

Next day, the Britons sent messengers to Caesar. They brought Commius the Gaul with them.

"We ask for peace, great Caesar," they said. "We are very sorry that some foolish persons tied the hands of your friend Commius. He is quite well now, as you see, and we ask for pardon."

Caesar sternly told them to tell their people to go back to their homes and fields. They must stop fighting and they must send their chiefs to the Roman camp.

18

Not long afterwards, a storm blew up and wrecked many of the Roman ships lying at anchor. Some of the ships that had been pulled up the beach were carried away by a high tide.

The Britons saw their chance. They made a sudden attack on a company of Roman soldiers who were out in the fields cutting corn. From the woods and marshes, a large force of Britons began to surround the camp.

As always, Caesar was ready for every danger. Ordering some of the soldiers to use the nails and planks from the wrecked ships to mend those that were less badly damaged, he led the rest of his army against the Britons and drove them off. Next day, he sailed back to Gaul.

Caesar was a great soldier. He had won many battles and he was not going back to Rome while men could say he had been beaten by the British tribesmen. He began to gather more soldiers and many ships.

Next year, all was ready. A larger force, with two thousand horses, landed on the coast of Kent but, this time, the Britons did not rush down to the beach. Their chief, Cassivellaunus, had made up his mind to fight inland.

As Caesar advanced from his camp on the shore, his troops were attacked by horsemen and by charioteers. They rode furiously at the Romans and then disappeared into the woods. This kind of fighting took place right across Kent, but Caesar pushed on steadily and crossed the River Thames at a ford where a sharp battle took place on the river bank.

Cassivellaunus could see that it was useless to fight battles against troops so steady and well-armed as the Romans. So he kept watch on their line of march, cut off any stragglers, burned the corn and drove off the cattle so the Romans became short of food. But Caesar captured the British stronghold near St. Albans and many of the tribes began to surrender.

After the men of Kent had failed in a surprise attack on the shore camp, Cassivellaunus sent envoys to Caesar to ask for peace.

"Tell Cassivellaunus," said Caesar, "that he must send corn and gold. This he shall pay to Rome every year. He shall promise not to harm Commius nor any of the chiefs who have made peace with me and, to make sure that he keeps his promise, he shall send me young men of noble birth who shall be hostages to his word."

As soon as the hostages arrived, Caesar marched back to the coast, for messengers had brought word that the Gauls were in revolt. The Romans and their prisoners went aboard the ships and within a few hours they had landed on the coast of Gaul.

Caesar never came back to Britain. After he had defeated the Gauls, he became ruler of Rome and of all the countries that border on the Mediterranean. He became so mighty that his enemies thought he wantedt obe king.

One day, when Caesar was in the Senate House, a man stepped up to him to ask a question. Suddenly, he pulled out a dagger. Caesar leapt back but found himself surrounded by men with knives. They stabbed him to death and ran out into the streets, crying, "Caesar is dead! Long live the Republic!"

Hostages on the march

The Emperor Hadrian

IN about the year 120, two soldiers of the Ninth Legion were polishing their armour in the barrack-room of the great fort at York:

"They say that the Emperor Hadrian is coming to Britain," said one.

"Then it will be drill, march and dig for us poor fellows," replied Otho the Gaul.

"What do you mean?" asked his companion.

"This Hadrian is made of iron. They say that his legs are never tired, for he walks all day, prying here, inspecting there. Everywhere he goes, he puts up new buildings and, most of all, he likes walls and ditches. There will be some digging to be done when he comes here, my friend."

"Why does he do this?"

"Gallus, the horse-dealer, who was in Germany buying horses for the cavalry, told me that when

22

Hadrian became Emperor after his uncle Trajan, he made up his mind that the Empire was big enough. He said that there would be no more wars. He means to build a wall all round the Empire and then the legions will have to keep the barbarians out."

"That's what we are here for, eh, Otho?"

"Right enough, Marcus. We march tonight to teach these wild Picts to mind their manners. Brr—but it's cold in this island!"

Marcus and Otho never came back to York. Somewhere in Scotland, the Ninth Legion was cut to pieces. Trapped perhaps in a glen, caught by a snow-storm or led into an ambush by a false guide, the Ninth was lost. A few officers and a handful of shivering men came back but no one ever knew what really happened to the proud legion. Worst of all, its Eagle Standard had vanished.

Not long after this terrible disgrace, the Emperor Hadrian arrived in Britain. He landed in Kent, at the port called Richborough, and he brought with him from Germany the Sixth Legion.

Travelling north on a broad firm road, Hadrian noted the signs of Roman law and order. He passed through new towns, with shops, market-places, public halls and baths. He saw fields of corn and sleek cattle; he passed merchants with waggons and pack-horses laden with hides, wool, iron and salt.

At York, the Emperor summoned the Roman commander and his chief officers to tell him about the loss of the Ninth Legion. He listened carefully and then he went himself to see something of this wild country whose tribesmen refused to be conquered. Bareheaded, he went everywhere on foot, walking at great speed, climbing rocks and hills to gain a view of the countryside, while his officers panted behind, cursing the rain and the cold which Hadrian seemed not to notice.

He visited the troops at their outlying forts, made them drill and throw their javelins, watched the cooks at work and sat down to eat the same food as the soldiers.

When he had seen all that he wanted, Hadrian called his officers together again. They looked curiously at this Emperor who never took any rest. He was broad-shouldered and of middle height, with a large nose and curly hair that lay thick on his forehead. Unlike most Emperors, he wore a short beard trimmed close to his cheeks and chin. His light-blue eyes had a strange far-away look and no one knew what he was thinking.

People said that Hadrian was a Spaniard but, although his family had lived in Spain for many years, he was proud of his Roman ancestors and he had spent much of his youth in Rome and Athens. Then he had travelled widely with his uncle Trajan, had fought in the wars and had seen more of the Roman Empire than any man alive. But he was more than a general and a peace-maker.

Hadrian addresses the officers at York

Hadrian was a painter, an architect and a poet. He put up many beautiful temples and theatres, he wrote verses and was the friend of artists, singers and writers. He helped the poor and the homeless, for he wished to win the love of the people, yet he could live as hard as any soldier on the frontier and sometimes he was as cruel as the barbarians themselves.

So the officers at York listened fearfully to this Emperor who was so clever and so strict:

"I have seen much in a short time," began Hadrian. "Your forts are good, your soldiers are well trained. I can praise their sword-work and their javelin-throwing, but there are some things I cannot praise. I will not speak much about the Ninth Legion. It

brought disgrace upon the name of Rome and, having lost its Eagle, it no longer exists. There is no Ninth Legion any more."

The officers gasped. A defeated legion was usually given fresh soldiers; sometimes it was moved to another part of the Empire. But this stern Emperor had wiped out the name of the Ninth.

"The Sixth Legion will take over the frontier," went on Hadrian. "Unroll the map, Florus. A wall is to be built from here to here. That is the shortest line from sea to sea. It measures seventy-six Roman miles. The wall is to be 10 feet thick and 20 feet high. In front there is to be a ditch 30 feet wide. I have given orders for the forts, signal-posts and turrets.

"From the wall, you will be able to control Caledonia. Peaceful traffic may pass freely through the gates. Your task is to protect the South from robbers and to put an end to the raids of the northern tribes. Inside my Empire, there must be peace."

Shortly afterwards, Hadrian left Britain to con-

tinue his travels, for there was much to be done in places more important than the small island on the edge of the Roman world. Men never understood him and he died near Rome, lonely and in pain, but he was perhaps the greatest of all the Emperors.

Parts of Hadrian's Wall can still be seen. It runs for mile after mile across the hills from Wallsend, near Newcastle, to Carlisle and the great ditch in front can still be traced. The wall was built of stone by the soldiers themselves. There was a walk along the top wide enough for two men to march abreast, and there were seventeen forts with "mile-castles" in between, each a mile apart and each with its gateway wide enough for a cart to pass through.

At least ten thousand soldiers dug the earth and lifted the stones into place. It took them five years. Later, the wall had to be altered and another line of forts was built farther away to the north. But, for two hundred and fifty years, Hadrian's Wall kept the Roman part of Britain safe from the fierce tribesmen of Caledonia.

27

Queen Ethelburga and Saint Paulinus

QUEEN Bertha of Kent carefully drew a gold thread through the cloth that lay on her lap. The cloak was finished and now she had begun to embroider its edges with a pattern of gold and scarlet.

As she sewed, the Queen talked to her little daughter Ethelburga, who was playing with her mother's bronze work-box on the bench where they sat together in the sunshine.

"Tell me, Mother, the story of Augustine," said the little princess.

"You know the story well, child, but I will tell it again," replied the Queen.

She told how she herself had crossed the sea from Gaul to marry Ethelbert, King of Kent. She loved her husband but she had been sad because he worshipped Thor and Woden. Bertha was a Christian, brought up in Paris, for her father was King of the Franks.

One day, Augustine had come to Kent, leading a band of forty monks who sang as they carried their silver cross over the flat fields to the place where King Ethelbert waited under an oak-tree with his nobles.

"For my sake," went on Queen Bertha, "your father said that he would listen to Augustine, though the priests of Woden were very angry. Afterwards, the King gave us the church of Saint Martin. It was in ruins then, but you know how pretty it is now, with its pink floor and the pictures of saints on the walls."

"But tell me how my father was made a Christian," said the little girl.

"Well, he pondered for a long time and then he said that he would be baptized. It was by the river. While the monks sang, Augustine blew in his face to drive away the bad spirits. Then he put salt in his mouth and led him into the river to dip him three times in the water. After that, the men of Kent were baptized too."

The child smiled, for this was one of her favourite stories. But it was time to go. She helped her mother to collect up the bronze needles and the threads of silk and wool, for the bell of Augustine's church was ringing for evening service.

Princess Ethelburga grew up happily at Canterbury. The land was peaceful, for Ethelbert was a wise ruler, obeyed by many under-kings beyond the borders of Kent. He was kind to Ethelburga when her mother died and he helped the monks to teach the people about God.

Suddenly, all was changed. Ethelbert died and his son Edwald became King. Edwald, with his fair beard, his loud laugh and his skill with axe and spear, was like one of the sea-pirates who had conquered Kent long ago. But he was also weak and lazy. When his father died, Edwald turned back to Thor and Woden, the old gods of the Saxon warriors.

The Church in Kent was almost overthrown. Some of the monks fled to Gaul, others went into hiding, but Archbishop Lawrence stayed at Canterbury, with Paulinus, a young priest from Italy, who acted as teacher to Princess Ethelburga.

The priests of Woden laughed and bowed to their idols. Feasts were held in the royal Hall and poets sang the praises of the young king who had brought back the old gods. Again and again, the Chief Priest told Edwald that he must banish his sister and kill the monks.

The good-natured Edwald stops his sister

But Edwald was fond of his sister. One day, as he came in from the hunt, he caught her by the wrist as she was going to her bower to say her prayers:

"Don't cry, little one," he roared in his good-natured way. "No one is going to hurt you. I won't send you away, but tell those Christian friends of yours to go while they are still alive."

"O brother, let these good men stay," pleaded Ethelburga. "Archbishop Lawrence cannot leave his flock and Paulinus is my friend. For the sake of our dear mother, let them stay."

"No, no," cried Edwald. "They must go tomorrow or they will die!"

Ethelburga ran to the place where she knew that she would find Paulinus and the archbishop. She told them that they must leave the kingdom at once.

"If only you could speak to my brother," she cried, "you would know that he is not really wicked.

The High Priest and some of the elders have led him away to the heathen gods. Perhaps God will tell us what to do."

That night, Lawrence dreamed that he saw Saint Peter himself. In the morning, Lawrence went to the Great Hall and demanded to speak with the King.

With shining eyes, Lawrence told Edwald that Saint Peter had appeared to him in a vision, telling him not to leave Kent. Disaster would come upon the kingdom if he left its shores but the fate of Edwald would be far more terrible if he did not return to the faith of his father and mother. Then the archbishop turned back his robe to show the King where Saint Peter had laid marks upon his back as a sign.

The young king fell on his knees and begged to be taken back into God's family. He promised that he would live as a Christian for the rest of his days.

Edwald kept his word. The monks came back from Gaul, the churches were open again and Ethelburga was able to go on helping the poor and teaching the children with the help of Paulinus.

Some time later, a messenger arrived at Canterbury. He came, he said, from Edwin, King of Northumbria, who sent words of greeting and gifts.

The royal messenger's servants brought in rich cloaks and tunics with gold wrist-clips, a pair of boar-hounds, arm-bracelets and a lady's work-box, inlaid with gold and precious stones. This last gift, said the messenger, was for the Princess Ethelburga. His royal master asked for her hand in marriage.

King Edwald stroked his beard and then answered slowly:

"Our thanks to Edwin for his noble gifts. We know him to be a great and valiant king, but we also know that he has not been baptized into the faith of Jesus Christ.

"Our sister is a Christian. If King Edwin would take her hand in marriage, he must promise not to hurt the Christian faith."

"O King," replied the messenger. "My master has bidden me to say that the fair princess may worship in her own way and her priests may speak of their God at all times. The King himself is ready to listen to the new teaching."

When he heard this, Edwald agreed that his sister could marry the northern King.

In the year 625, Ethelburga set out from Canterbury with Paulinus and a helper named James the Deacon. Maids, servants and a strong bodyguard travelled with them.

It was a long journey, across hills and rivers, along woodland tracks where only a guide could tell the way. The princess rode behind a servant. Often she walked and sometimes, where the road was deep with mud, she had to be carried.

King Edwin was overlord to the Middle Angles and the East Angles, so their spearmen rode out to meet the princess. Each night, they brought her to a royal manor where she dined and rested.

At last, the travellers reached the Great Hall of Edwin. The King came forward to greet his bride, taking both her hands in his and kissing her upon each cheek. Then his eyes turned to the tall, dark stranger who stood beside the fair-haired girl. He started with fear:

"Who is this man, princess?" he cried.

"He is Paulinus, my lord," answered Ethelburga. "A man of God who has travelled with me to your northern land according to your promise."

"Paulinus? I have seen his thin, dark face before. Now I remember. It was long ago, when I was homeless, a man without land or followers, and I saw in a dream this dark man. He gave me a sign and told me that I should be great one day. Was it you stranger? Do you recall the sign?"

Paulinus looked keenly at the King but he did not answer. Slowly he raised his hand and placed it on the King's head. The nobles stared. Surely the King would be angry, but Edwin stood quite still.

"Yes, that was the sign I saw in my vision," he murmured.

King Edwin was a strong, hard man. His life had been full of adventure and fighting but now that he had won back his father's kingdom, he meant to rule well with his Kentish bride to help him.

From the moment he saw her, Edwin loved

Ethelburga travels north to marry Edwin

Ethelburga and granted all her wishes. Her gentle manner, her pity for the poor and her strange religion filled him with wonder. Her way of speaking, her dress and her skilful needlework made her different from the northern ladies and, unlike them, she could read and could sing most beautifully. Every day, she and Paulinus prayed and sang together but, so far, Edwin took no interest in their religion.

About a year after the royal wedding, a man named Eomer came to the court with a message from the King of the West Saxons. There had been a quarrel between the two rulers but, even so, Eomer was taken to the Great Hall where Edwin sat with his nobles. The messenger knelt and opened his cloak as if to present a gift or a letter.

At that moment, the thane Lilla, standing by the King's seat, flung himself forward as Eomer aimed a dagger at the King's heart. So strong was the blow that the blade passed through Lilla's body and wounded Edwin. A dozen hands struck down Eomer, but Lilla was already dead. He had saved the King's life.

That same evening, Ethelburga's first baby was born, a girl who was named Eanfled. King Edwin was filled with thankfulness and he sent for Paulinus:

"The Queen, my lady wife, says that my life was saved by your prayers to the Christian God. She wishes our new-born child to be the first Christian to be baptized in Northumbria."

Paulinus asked the King if he remembered the vision and the sign. Edwin spoke again:

"When my wound is healed, I shall march against the West Saxons. If I am given victory, I too will become a Christian."

After the baby had been baptized, the King and his warriors set out to punish the King of Wessex. The two armies met on a bare hillside where the Northumbrian axes cut through the enemy ranks and the spearmen finished the victory.

At home again, Edwin kept his promise. He called together the earls and the wise men of the kingdom and told them that he wished them to listen to Paulinus.

The tall priest told how Jesus had chosen pain and death, how He had won the battle with death and had risen gloriously to open the door of God's kingdom to all who had the courage to follow Him.

With burning words, Paulinus went on to explain why Christians believed that mercy and kindness were better than hate and cruel revenge. He also spoke about life after death.

When he had finished, the warriors and the old men looked silently at the stranger who stood unarmed in their midst, a man who had come to them from far-off Italy because he believed in a God so different from the heathen gods.

At last, the King asked a white-bearded counsellor to speak. The old man rose:

Coifi hurls his spear at the idol of Woden

"The life of a man, O King," he said, "is like the flight of a sparrow through the Hall when we sit at meat in winter time with the fire blazing. It flies in through one door and quickly out of the other. For a little while, it is safe from the storm but soon it vanishes into the winter again.

"Our life is like the sparrow. Where he came from and where he goes we know not. If Paulinus can tell us these things, we should follow his teaching."

Then Coifi, the High Priest, sprang up and cried:

"I am telling the truth, O King, when I say that our gods are useless. No one has served them better than I, but they have brought me no luck or favour. Give me, I beg, a straight spear and a horse and I will show what should be done to the old gods."

When he was mounted, Coifi rode furiously to the temple and hurled his spear at the idol of Woden. Then he called to the people to burn down the temple, for Northumbria was to be a Christian kingdom.

Paulinus and James the Deacon hurried to build a little wooden church at York and here, amid the ruins of the Roman city, Edwin and his court were baptized.

Once the King had become a Christian, the people came flocking to listen to Paulinus. He and James tramped all over Northumbria, teaching and baptizing the crowds who gathered on the banks of streams and rivers to receive the blessing of God.

Edwin was now the most powerful king in England. When he went out with his Queen to see that the land was well ruled, his banners were carried in front of him. Men said that the realm was so peaceful that a woman with her baby could walk from sea to sea in safety.

At York, King Edwin gave orders for a church of stone to be built, but before its walls were finished, he lay dead on a battlefield.

Penda, the heathen ruler of Mercia, helped by a Welsh king, attacked Northumbria, wiped out its army and carried the dead King's head on a spear into York. The victors tore across the land like a gale, killing and burning as they went.

When the terrible news of the battle reached Ethelburga, she fled with her daughter to Paulinus. For a time they were safe, but soon they had to flee to the coast.

What should Paulinus do? His churches were destroyed, the King was dead and the heathens

were killing Christians wherever they found them. The way to the South was barred by the enemy and, in any case, there were no troops to guard the royal travellers.

At last, Paulinus found a sea-captain who was sailing back to Gaul because, as he said, there was no trade when men were afraid to come out of doors. For a handful of gold, he would take the priest and his friends on board his ship.

James the Deacon bravely declared that he would stay, so Ethelburga, her daughter and Paulinus sailed away from Northumbria and, after many days, were put ashore on the coast of Kent.

King Edwald gave a kind welcome to his sister. He was not strong enough to march against the savage Penda but he thought of a plan that might bring happiness to Ethelburga.

At Lyminge, there was a royal manor with good pastures where fat sheep were raised. It was big enough to provide the food and money that were needed to support a small abbey. Edwald gave the manor of Lyminge to his sister.

Here, with her daughter, Ethelburga spent the rest of her life in the quiet countryside of Kent. She lived in a little house by herself and there were separate buildings for the nuns and for the young girls called novices. There was a chapel, a dining-room, a hospital for the sick and a house for Paulinus and for the monks who came to join him.

Ethelburga's manor at Lyminge

Ethelburga and Paulinus never went back to York. Often, when they met in the garden at Lyminge, they would talk of their journey to Northumbria, of the miracle of King Edwin's conversion, and of the five happy years before he was killed in battle. Many times they spoke of James the Deacon and wondered if he was still alive.

One day, a traveller brought the good news that James had managed to go on teaching a few Christians in secret until a prince named Oswald had driven Penda out. Then Saint Aidan had come from Iona to bring back Christianity to Northumbria.

Ethelburga was happy.

"Our work was not wasted, Paulinus," she cried. "The word of God will never again die out in Northumbria."

St. Cuthbert of Durham

"CARELESS rascals," growled the old shepherd, "throwing stones instead of minding the flock. What will the master do to ye when he knows that one of his fine sheep is trapped in a cleft on a rock-face where a fly could hardly crawl?"

"I'll fetch her down," cried the tallest of the three shepherd-boys.

"You, Cuthbert?" said the old shepherd. "Well, ye may try. But it's your neck that will be broken."

The boy laughed and began to climb the steep rock-face. Bits of rock broke away under his bare feet. Once he almost fell but he held on by his finger-nails until his toes found a tiny ledge to stand on.

He climbed until he reached the place where one of the sheep was wedged in the rocks. Then he lifted the animal out, set it on its feet and followed it up to the hillside above.

By an easier path, Cuthbert brought the sheep back to the flock. The old shepherd grunted and the boys grinned their thanks. They knew Cuthbert. He was as hard and whippy as a leather thong and he loved to test his strength in ways that were too difficult for them.

By nightfall, the flocks had been brought to an open space by a small river. The shepherds lit a fire and ate their bread and bacon. Then, while one kept watch, the others curled themselves to sleep in the shelter of the boulders.

When it was his turn, Cuthbert went up to a higher patch of ground from which he could see the sheep all round him. The night was cold and very still and the sky was a dark bowl filled with stars.

Cuthbert shivered. He remembered the prayers that Kenwith the Widow had taught him. She had looked after him since the time when his mother died and his father had been killed fighting the Mercians. He was on his knees praying when he saw the great light.

Far off, yet brilliantly clear, a globe of fire passed across the sky and in it the boy saw what seemed to be a company of angels rising upwards to Heaven. What could it be? Was it a sign, perhaps for him alone? He stood up. The shepherds were still asleep, the sheep were quiet, but Cuthbert knew that he had seen a vision.

A few days later, Cuthbert was telling his story to Basil, prior of the monastery at Melrose.

"Yes, my son," said the prior gravely, "on that very night, Bishop Aidan died at Lindisfarne. What you saw was that holy man's soul being carried to Heaven. It is a sign that you are called to do God's work."

The prior went to see Cuthbert's master to ask if the lad could enter the monastery. The thane shook his head:

"No, Father. Our King has called me to raise a hundred spearmen for the royal army of Northumbria. The lad Cuthbert is sixteen, tall and strong for his age. He will be doing God's work by keeping the kingdom safe from the heathen Mercians. But if he lives, I promise that he shall enter your house."

So Cuthbert, mounted on a shaggy pony, followed his lord to war. For two years, he carried his spear against the Mercians and he knew what it was to live hard, to ride all night and to go into battle at dawn.

At last, the fighting came to an end and Cuthbert went to speak to his lord:

"I made a vow to enter the Church, master," he said. "May I now leave your service?"

The thane looked at the young man:

Cuthbert goes to war against the Mercians

"You have served me well and I would not lose so good a man. But a promise was given. Go, in Christ's name. Is it to Lindisfarne you go?"

"No, master. I know that Aidan's church has many holy men. But the prior Basil has been my friend. I will go to Melrose."

When Cuthbert reached Melrose, he gave his horse and his spear to the servant who opened the gate. Basil welcomed him and said that he must go to see Eata, the abbot.

"So you would turn from war to be a monk?" asked Eata. "I have heard of the vision that God showed you. But there is much for you to learn. Can you read?"

"Not yet, Father. But I will learn."

"So you shall, my son, and I will be your teacher."

The shepherd-lad learned quickly and the other monks at Melrose came to look on him as a natural leader. He was so strong that they chose him to be the chief builder, but since he was kind and friendly, they also chose him to look after the guests and travellers who stayed at the monastery.

When Basil died, the monks asked Eata if Cuthbert could be their prior. He lived at Melrose for several years and there were many stories of his adventures.

Cuthbert was not content to stay quietly inside the monastery walls. He made many a journey north-wards into the wild land of the Picts. There he would search out the tribesmen, follow them to their mountain homes and baptize them in the name of Jesus.

The fierce Picts liked the preacher who had been a soldier and was afraid of no one. He had the gift of healing sick people and a wonderful way with horses and wild creatures.

Once, he and two of the brothers from Melrose crossed the Firth of Forth in a storm. Drenched to the skin, dog-tired and hungry, they dragged their little boat out of reach of the waves and saw, waiting for them on the shore, three portions of dolphin's flesh.

On another occasion, returning from a journey to heal a sick woman, Cuthbert and his fellows lost their way and were all day without food until an

*Cuthbert and his friends drag their boat ashore and find
three portions of dolphin flesh*

eagle brought them a large fish. The monks told how
Cuthbert made them give half of the fish to the eagle
for its own dinner.

The monks also told of the time when Cuthbert
was praying on the sea-shore. It was bitterly cold and
they saw two little seals come up out of the sea to
lick and warm his frozen feet.

When Eata was made a bishop, he sent Cuthbert
to the famous monastery at Lindisfarne, an island
off the coast of Northumbria. After a time, Cuthbert
told the monks that he must leave them:

"I would be alone with God," he said.

"But, here on Lindisfarne, you can rest and pray,"
cried the monks.

"Truly," replied Cuthbert, "it is peaceful here in Aidan's house. There is shelter from the sea-wind and warmth in the sunshine by the wall. But I do not seek shelter and warmth. As the Saint hath said, 'Go ye bare. As Christ had nothing, so shall ye have nothing.' "

So Cuthbert went to live alone on the isle of Farne, one of a group of tiny islands, nine miles from Lindisfarne. There he dug down into the earth to make a space to dwell in and he built an outer wall, moving by himself great stones that four of the brothers could not have lifted.

At this time, people looked on hermits as holy men. On fine days, the monks of Lindisfarne would row across to Farne to visit their brother. They would find him in his cell, surrounded by a wall so that he could only see the sky. Often they found him praying and they would go away without a word, leaving some food outside his cell.

While Cuthbert was following this lonely way of life, there was no bishop of Lindisfarne. At last, the King of Northumbria called a meeting of the clergy and, with one voice, they chose Cuthbert.

Then a party set out by boat to the tiny island. They called to Cuthbert to speak with them and, when he would not answer, they drew him up gently out of his cell and asked him to be their bishop:

"Your brothers implore you with tears to come back," they cried.

Cuthbert in his cell is visited by the monks

At this, Cuthbert yielded. The monks rowed him to the mainland and led him to the meeting where, in the presence of the King, the Archbishop held the service by which the hermit of Farne became Bishop of Lindisfarne.

After many years, Cuthbert fell ill and knew that he was going to die. He asked a few of the brothers to take him for the last time to his cell on the little island:

"I wish to be buried there," he said.

But the brothers begged to be allowed to arrange his burying-place in the church at Lindisfarne. Cuthbert spoke again:

"You may do so. But, remember this: if wicked men come to rule this land, I ask you to take my bones and go to whatever place God may lead you."

Cuthbert died on the Farne island in March 687 and the monks buried him by the side of the altar at Lindisfarne.

A hundred years passed. Then, one day, a band of Danish raiders burnt the monastery and killed many of the monks. Cuthbert's tomb escaped the fire and,

after the raiders had gone, monks came out from the mainland to rebuild the monastery.

Another eighty years went by and the heathen Danes were conquering all the kingdoms of the north and east. One by one, the monasteries of Northumbria were robbed and burnt. At Lindisfarne, Bishop Erdwulf spoke sadly to the monks:

"Brothers, the time has come when we should remember Saint Cuthbert's dying words. He told us not to live under wicked masters but to take his bones from this place."

Without delay, the monks crossed to the mainland, taking with them Cuthbert's coffin and the Lindisfarne Gospels that had been written and decorated so gloriously in his honour. Seven young priests carried the coffin on their shoulders, and later it was placed on a cart drawn by a bay horse.

For seven years, the bishop and the monks and a little band of Christians wandered about trying to find a resting-place safe from the Danes. At last, in despair, they decided to take the coffin to Ireland where the Irish Christians would give it shelter.

Bishop, abbot and bearers went aboard a ship that was lying in the mouth of the River Derwent. When the sails were set, the rest of the company stood on the shore, weeping:

"Do not leave us," they wailed. "Stay with us, Cuthbert, in our time of need!"

A storm arose with waves so violent that the ship was driven back. Then the bishop ordered the coffin to be carried ashore. The Saint had made it clear that his bones were not to leave the kingdom.

The company set out on their wanderings again and came to Chester-le-Street in the county of Durham. Because his people could travel no further, the bishop said that all must settle there.

With the Danes not far away at York, the Christians had an anxious time for many years. They lived in fear and, time after time, they seemed to be doomed. But somehow they were saved and their church still stood. People felt sure that Saint Cuthbert was their protector in the North.

Indeed, everyone said that it was with Saint Cuthbert's help that King Alfred defeated the Danes in Wessex. Then Alfred's grandson, the great Athelstan, travelled to the North to visit the Saint's tomb and to make the Danes promise to be Christians.

So, in 995, the day came when it was safe to move Saint Cuthbert's coffin to Durham where it has rested ever since.

The Venerable Bede

"COME, my son," said Abbot Benedict, taking the hand of the small boy who was following him through the monastery gate, "this is your home now. Here, at St. Peter's, you can grow up in God's keeping."

The good abbot took the boy first into the church, where the child's eyes lit up with wonder at the bright pictures of saints on the walls and at the glass windows, newly brought from Gaul. Presently, the abbot paused to speak to a monk, who was carefully painting a great capital letter at the head of a page

53

of the book that he was copying. The boy hung back and seemed unwilling to go on to see the gardens and the kitchens where other monks were working.

"What is it?" asked the abbot. "Does the book interest you?"

"I have never seen a book before, Father," answered the boy. "Will I have one when I learn to read?"

"You shall have many books, my son, if you work hard at your lessons."

The boy's name was Bede. He was only seven years old when both his parents died and the kind-hearted abbot brought him to live at the monastery at Wearmouth in Northumbria, not far from the Roman Wall of Hadrian. In the year 680, monasteries were the only places where orphans and sick people could find peace and safety. They were the only places, too, where boys could learn to read and write.

Young Bede was happy at Wearmouth. He helped in the kitchen and the bakery, he ran errands and he learned to sing with the monks in the great church. Most of all, he enjoyed his lessons. Soon, the prior was able to tell the abbot that the little orphan was very clever:

"The boy learns so fast that there are not enough

books for him to read. Already, he reads Latin and
Greek as easily as the birds fly."

"Books are precious," replied the abbot, "but I
promised on the day when he came here that he
should have them. I will make a journey to find
books for this boy, for it is clear that God has chosen
him to be a great scholar."

Abbot Benedict was as good as his word. He set
out to ride from one monastery to another; he
crossed to France and travelled to Italy and back to
the Low Countries searching always for books
which he might buy or borrow for the library of
his monastery in the north of England. As he had
said, books were precious. Each one had to be
copied by hand on sheets of parchment and almost
all of them were written in Greek or Latin and some
were in the Hebrew language.

Young Bede helping in the bakery

After several years, the abbot returned to Northumbria with a wonderful collection of books strapped carefully to the pack-horses that clattered into the abbey courtyard. The monks welcomed their abbot joyfully and, in the church that evening, the voice of the boy Bede could be heard high above the others as he sang his gladness that his friend had come home bringing so many books filled with knowledge.

By this time, Bede was living at Jarrow, at the monastery of St. Paul, which Abbot Benedict had founded before he went on his travels.

When Bede was fourteen, an illness, called the plague, came to Jarrow and so many of the monks fell ill and died that there was no one left to take the services in the church, except the prior and Bede. The singing was too difficult for the monks who were being trained to take the place of those who had died, so the prior and the boy sang alone, each taking his turn, until the new monks had learned their parts.

After this, the monastery at Jarrow grew larger. Its library of books collected by the abbot became so famous that scholars came from abroad to visit it, and nobles sent their sons there to be taught by the monks. Bede himself became a monk after he had grown up and men began to say that he was not only the wisest man in England but the best scholar in Europe.

Bede teaching his pupils

In those days, clever men spent most of their time studying the Scriptures and the writings of Rome and Ancient Greece. Bede was interested in everything, in music, history and nature, as well as in the Scriptures. Soon he began to write books himself.

He wrote not only about saints and the early history of the Church, but also about science, grammar, the stars and his own two monasteries. Much of his writing was done to help the boys and the young monks who came thronging to Jarrow, for he remembered how much he had longed for books when he was a boy.

So many people wanted to send their sons to Bede that he started a school. There were six hundred pupils, many from France, Spain and Italy. They came great distances to Jarrow to be taught by the quiet monk who was always too busy himself to go on journeys, except to visit his friends at neighbouring monasteries.

One day, when he was walking in the garden, his friend Nothelm spoke lovingly of the school and of the books which Bede had written for the boys:

"There is one book, brother, above all others that I would like to write," said Bede.

"What is this book?"

"It is a book about the history of the Church in England," replied Bede. "I would tell how the Word of God came to our shores and spread over the land. I would have our boys know the stories of the saints and of great happenings long ago."

"Of all men, you can surely write such a book," cried Nothelm.

"No, brother, I have never travelled and know little of the happenings in the Kingdom of Kent or in East Anglia or Wessex. I cannot leave my school and my books to find out the history of those places."

"But there are those who will help you. You alone can write this book but others can bring you the things you need to know. I myself was a monk in Kent and there is Brother Albinus of Canterbury, a far more learned man than I. There is Bishop Daniel to send word of the West Saxons; there are Wilfred and Acca who have travelled far and John who was long in Rome.

Bede writing his history of the Church

"All these and many others will bring you books and writings from distant monasteries. You must write your history of the Church."

So it was that Bede wrote the first great history book in England. His friends helped, but it was Bede, the story-teller, who told so beautifully how Christianity came to Northumbria, how Caedmon the cowherd received the gift of poetry, how Cuthbert and many others served God. To Bede, we owe most of our knowledge of what happened in those far-off days.

The history of England took a long time to write, and when it was finished Bede was growing old. There was one more task he meant to do:

"All my books have been written in Latin," he said. "The common people cannot understand them, so I will translate the Gospel of Saint John into their tongue, so that when it is read to them, they can understand."

The monks were very surprised that a great scholar should think of turning the Scriptures into Anglo-Saxon, but Bede was already at work. He seemed to know that his life was nearly over for he wrote all day for as long as daylight lasted. When he became too ill to hold his pen, a young monk acted as his scribe, sitting at his bedside in his little cell. In the evenings, when it was too dark to write any more, the old man would chant the songs that he knew so well and think about the book that was almost finished.

On the Feast of the Ascension, all the monks went to take part in the procession round the church, but Bede could not leave his bed. He was alone with the scribe.

"We must begin, Wilbert," he said, "I do not want my boys to have to finish this when I am dead and I do not want them to read what is untrue."

"But, master, there is only one chapter to write. Rest now, for it is too difficult for you to speak."

"No, it is easy. Take thy pen and write quickly."

Making all haste, the young man wrote down the words of his dying master. All day they continued and as the sun began to sink, Bede paused and smiled at several of his friends who had gathered in the cell. He made a little gift to each one and then turned to his scribe:

"Where are we, my son?" he asked.

"There is one more sentence to write, dear master."

"Then write quickly what I tell you."

Presently, the monk laid down his pen and sighed happily:

"Now, it is finished."

"Thou hast spoken truly," said Bede. "All is finished."

Then he asked his friends to carry him to his usual place of prayer. They helped him to kneel down and after he had prayed, he sang a little and they carried him, still singing, back to his cell. He did not wake next morning and the monks buried him at Jarrow where he had worked so well for almost all his life.

Bede was mourned far and wide and when the news of his death reached Germany, an English monk who was working there to convert the heathen Saxons, wrote to tell his friends at Jarrow that Bede's name "shone like a candle in the church".

Men spoke of him as the "Venerable Bede", for "venerable" meant "worthy of respect and love". For many years, pilgrims came to pray at his grave and sick children were brought to be cured at Bede's Well. Three hundred years after his death, his bones were taken to Durham Cathedral where his tomb can still be seen in the Galilee chapel.

The Saxon Minster at York

Alcuin of York

IN the year that Bede died at Jarrow, a baby boy was born in York. He was named Alcuin and, when he was quite small, he was sent to the Cathedral School.

His teacher was Aelbert, and after the boy had been going to his lessons for some months the school was visited by Archbishop Egbert. The archbishop listened to the boys as they answered their teachers:

"The work is well done," he said to Aelbert. "Some of the thanes' sons are very slow but I see one who learns more easily than the others."

"That is Alcuin, Father," said Aelbert. "He is my best pupil. Sometimes I think that he will be a scholar as famous as our beloved Bede."

"It is hard to believe that anyone could be as clever as Bede. But you may be right. Give the boy all the help that he needs and let him see something of the world as well as the schoolroom."

Aelbert remembered this advice and when Alcuin was older he took him to Rome. It was a long journey across Frankland but the boy and his master stayed at monasteries along the way where they were always given a kind welcome.

When he came back from his travels, Alcuin stayed on at the Cathedral School. He read many books about the Church and the Bible and he also learnt the seven subjects that were taught in those days. They were arithmetic, music, geometry, grammar, astronomy and two others called rhetoric (speaking aloud) and dialect (holding a learned argument).

In all these, Alcuin was so clever that he began to teach some of the younger boys and, later, he took charge of the whole school. He was called Master of Scholars.

A few years passed and Alcuin might have stayed at York for the rest of his life. But, one day, his old teacher Aelbert, now Archbishop of York, came to see him:

"Alcuin, my son," he said, "I want you to make the journey to Rome. Are you willing to go?"

"Yes, indeed, Father," answered Alcuin. "I shall be able to see so many places that we visited when I

was a boy. And I can call upon some of my former pupils who live in foreign monasteries. But I forget myself. What is the purpose of the journey?"

"You know that the Pope gives the 'pallium' to every archbishop. That wide scarf of white woollen cloth is the sign of his holy office. I would have you fetch my pallium from the hands of His Holiness in Rome."

Joyfully, Alcuin gathered together the few things necessary for his journey. Then, with two monks for company, he crossed in a merchant ship to the Low Countries, travelled down the Rhine Valley and across the mountains into Italy.

The Pope welcomed the English scholar and Alcuin spent several weeks visiting churches and talking to the scholars of the Holy City. Then it was time to say good-bye and to set out on the long journey home, carrying the precious pallium and several baskets of books.

One evening, he and his companions came to Parma in North Italy. There were crowds of people and a great deal of noise in the town.

"What is happening today in Parma, brother?" asked Alcuin of the monk who let him in at the gate of the small religious house where he was to stay the night.

Celebrations during Charles' visit to Parma

"Have you not heard," replied the monk, "that Charles, King of the Franks, is here? Unlike you, my friend, King Charles does not travel quietly. Thousands of soldiers, hundreds of serving-men, cooks, scullions, merchants, jugglers, minstrels, poets, women, children, scribes, rascals and cut-throats— they all go along with the Frankish Court.

"Oh, you never saw so many people in your life! But come in now, good friends, our prior waits to welcome you at our table. We have heard, here in this little priory, of Alcuin of York."

Next morning, a messenger in a splendid blue cloak knocked at the priory gate. He had come, he said, from Charles, King of the Franks. His royal master had heard that a famous English scholar was in the town and he asked with deep respect if the Englishman would go and talk with him.

Alcuin cheerfully agreed and followed the messenger to where a two-wheeled cart awaited them. Presently, they came to the abbey where the King and his family were staying.

Alcuin was led into the hall and at once the King rose and came to meet him, throwing his arms wide in welcome. To Alcuin's astonishment, he was hugged like a bear and half-carried to the seat where the King had been sitting.

When Alcuin had got his breath back, he looked closely at this jovial king. Charles was enormous, a giant of a man, taller than any of his knights and twice as wide. Men said that he was so strong that he could break an iron horseshoe in halves like a dry stick, and lift a man in full armour above his head, with one hand.

The king was as jolly as a schoolboy. His blue eyes twinkled under bushy eyebrows and he chuckled away into a great fair beard that flowed on to his vast chest. Yet when he spoke, he had a high piping voice.

"Come, Father, sit by me," he cried to Alcuin. "Long have I wished to speak with the scholar of York. A king should know many things but I have little learning. There is much that I would have you teach me."

With a boy's eagerness, Charles asked question after question. The evening passed. Dinner was served at the high table, the knights dropped asleep

Charles welcomes Alcuin to his court

over their wine, the women slipped away to their bowers and the servants and guards stood drowsily in the shadows of the hall. But still the King sat with Alcuin, talking and asking questions.

In the weeks that followed, Charles could hardly bear to be away from Alcuin. The noisy Court left Parma and made its way slowly towards Frankland, with the King riding beside Alcuin, deep in talk with his new friend.

When they reached Frankland, Charles said to Alcuin:

"Father, I know that you must return to England. But I beg you to come back. You shall be Master of my Palace School and shall make it as famous as York. There is much to be done in Frankland, for we have few schools and much ignorance, even among the clergy."

Alcuin promised that, when he had taken the pallium safely to York, he would ask for permission to live in Frankland.

To his surprise, Alcuin found that the Archbishop and the King of Northumbria were willing to let him go. It would be good, they felt, to have the King of the Franks for a friend. Already, men were calling him Charlemagne or Charles the Great.

So Alcuin went back to Frankland to live at the King's Court. He found that Charles ruled everything and everybody like the father of a big family. He looked into the law-courts, the farms, manors,

Charles rides with a group of scholars
while on the march

monasteries, market-squares and even into the
cooking-pots in the peasants' huts. Nothing escaped
his sharp, twinkling eyes.

Alcuin came to love this huge, chuckling king
who was so eager to learn and to do good. Charles
would not waste a minute of the day. As soon as he
woke, he sent for friends to talk to him while he
dressed. At meals, he liked to hear music or to have
a book read aloud. On the march, he rode with a
group of scholars, talking to them and asking
questions.

Yet Charles was full of fun. Sometimes he would
stop by a river and order everyone to join him in a
swim—courtiers, monks, ambassadors, everyone.

He loved children and was so fond of his three pretty daughters that he could not bear to lose them. When they grew up and were married, they still had to live at Court so that Charles could kiss them every morning.

In this lively kingdom, Alcuin found that there was a great deal of work to do. Even in the monasteries, many of the monks could barely read and write and the books were full of mistakes because they had been badly copied by monks who did not understand Latin very well.

First of all, Alcuin started a Palace School. The Frankish nobles were fighting-men who liked nothing better than riding to war behind the banners of their King, but they cared little for reading and writing. Now their sons had to go to school. Some of these proud youngsters, in their fur-trimmed tunics and boots of soft leather, were very lazy. Once, Charles found them admiring a hawk instead of paying attention:

"By the King of Heaven," he roared, "I care nothing for your fine looks and noble birth. Know this, unless you make up for your lazy ways, you will get nothing from Charles!"

It was among the poorer boys that Alcuin found his best scholars. When they were old enough, they went as teachers to the abbey schools that he started and, in time, some of them became bishops and abbots.

Charles is furious with the nobles' sons for admiring a hawk instead of studying

Alcuin and Charles spread knowledge throughout Frankland. They remained great friends, although they were so different, the masterful king and the quiet-spoken scholar.

Charles could be very cruel. He was a Christian and he tried to convert the heathen Saxons of Germany. With fire and slaughter, he forced them to worship Jesus Christ and he made them pay heavily for the churches that he built in their fireswept land.

Alcuin spoke sharply to the King:

"You love the truth but you do evil. It would have been better if the Saxons had been told about the love of Christ, instead of being forced by hard punishments."

Charles was not angry. He loved his friend all the more for speaking out boldly. In time, he came to

71

realize that he ought to have treated the Saxons more kindly.

Alcuin's work went on. He lived at the great palace which Charles built when he grew tired of wandering about with his Court. The Palace School was a splendid building, but Alcuin did not forget England. He went back on a long visit, partly to see his old friends and partly to patch up a quarrel between Charles and Offa, King of Mercia.

Alcuin loved the bustle of the Frankish Court and the work of being Charles' adviser but, as he grew old, he wanted peace and time to think about God.

Charles loved him too much to let him go far away, so he gave him the Abbey of Tours, a monastery so big that its lands were worked by twenty thousand serfs.

Here, as Abbot, Alcuin spent the last years of his life, still busy with a school and with the books that he was constantly writing. But there was time to walk in the gardens, to think and to listen to the birds. Charles often came to see him and, between visits, they wrote to each other about every subject under the sun.

In the year 800, Alcuin was not well enough to make the journey to Rome where Charles was crowned Emperor. He stayed on at Tours, among the flowers and trees. He died there in the spring, when the birds, especially the cuckoo that so delighted him, were returning to his garden.

Ethelfleda

THE LADY OF THE MERCIANS

"COME, daughter, sit here in the window-seat," said King Alfred. "Will you listen while I tell you how you can help me and the kingdom?"

Ethelfleda looked up from her embroidery:

"Father," she said, "I will try all my life to serve Wessex in the way that you have taught us."

The King smiled a little sadly. He loved his eldest child and it was not easy to tell her that she must soon leave her home and her brothers and sisters.

"You know, child, how God gave me the victory

73

over the Danes? How, after all seemed lost, the men of Wessex defeated the pagan host and how Guthrum the Dane was baptized at Wedmore?"

"Yes, Father," answered Ethelfleda, "I know that you forgave your enemies and they promised to go away and leave our land in peace."

"True, Wessex was saved and Guthrum has not broken his word. But the Danes were hungry for land and when they failed to take Wessex, they cast their eyes upon Mercia, the kingdom next to our own.

"Knowing that the Northmen would fall upon them, the Mercians turned to me, for their own king was a poor creature, not a man but a trembling puppet. The greatest of the Mercian earls is Aethelred and to him I gave the lands of western Mercia and the valley of the Severn."

"Then Mercia is safe, Father? What have I to do?"

"I will tell you, my daughter. Your mother was a Mercian princess, and your aunt was Queen of Mercia before she and her husband were forced to flee abroad. Yet there are many Mercians who do not trust me. They think that I would take their land, that Alfred is now a bigger foe than Guthrum.

"Wessex and Mercia must stand together or both will fall. To show my friendship and to make a bond between the two kingdoms, I would give my daughter in marriage to Earl Aethelred. What say you, will you marry Aethelred?"

England at the
time of
Ethelfleda

The coloured
areas were
controlled by
the Danes

Ethelfleda bent over her embroidery to hide her tears. She was only sixteen and she knew that Aethelred was almost as old as her own father. She had heard, too, that long ago a Danish axe had split his war-helmet and gashed his face so that it was terrible to look at.

"I will do as my father bids me," she whispered.

"It is not my way to drive those who are weak, much less those who are dear to me. Do you go willingly?"

Ethelfleda raised her head proudly:

"I am your daughter, Father. I will marry Aethelred because you ask me to do so."

75

Ethelfleda meets her future husband, Earl Aethelred

So, with an escort of Wessex nobles, Ethelfleda rode into Mercia and was married to Earl Aethelred in a wooden church by the River Severn. She saw at once that the tale of his injury was true. A terrible scar ran from his forehead to his chin, splitting one eyebrow and giving him a savage expression. But his voice was gentle:

"You honour me greatly, Ethelfleda," he said. "My people and I have given our hearts to the daughter of noble Alfred."

It was true. The Earl and the Mercian folk loved the fair-haired princess from Wessex who rode to the hunt like a man, who could equal any boy with the bow and yet was as clever with her books as she was kind to the poor and the sick.

For her part, Ethelfleda was happy. She came to admire her tall, scarred husband so much that she could not bear to be parted from him. She rode everywhere with him about the kingdom, seeing to its defences, talking to the earls and the men-at-arms, the farm people and the children. To them, she was no longer a stranger. She was their own first lady in the land and they called her, "The Lady of the Mercians".

Two years after Ethelfleda's marriage, when her baby daughter was still in her cradle, a great fleet of more than 800 ships brought a fresh host of Danes to the shores of Kent and Essex. Led by Hasting, their chief, they made raids across England into the heart of Mercia, where they reached the Severn Valley and laid it waste with fire. But the Mercians would not give in.

With Ethelfleda at his side, the Earl kept his men in the field, hanging on to the fringe of the host, cutting down stragglers and giving the enemy no rest. Alfred and the men of Wessex came up from the south and also struck hard at the Danish bases near the Thames.

The invaders were baffled. Was this the soft land they had heard of? Was this the country where rich farmland and fat cattle were to be had for the taking? They pushed inland as far as the Welsh border and wintered at Chester. But although they came out of camp in the spring to burn and kill with their usual horrible zest, there was no sign that the Englishmen would allow them to settle in the land.

At last, after three years of warfare, Hasting gave up the struggle and took his host back to Frankland. Aethelred and his lady set to work to rebuild their shattered villages and King Alfred was able to live in peace for the rest of his reign.

Alfred died and his son Edward became King of Wessex. At once, the troubles broke out again. A jealous cousin fled to the north where he made friends with the Yorkshire Danes and with Eric of East Anglia whose armies came raiding as far south as Wiltshire.

They were driven back but next spring they came again and the year after that. The struggle swayed to and fro across Mercia, a buffer land crossed by armies, until the countryside became a waste of blackened fields and roofless cottages.

Ethelfleda naturally turned for help to her brother Edward. Then the Mercians, fighting shoulder to shoulder with the men of Wessex, crushed the Danish host in a great battle in Staffordshire.

But Aethelred was not there with his army. A strange illness had taken away his strength and

A messenger brings news of Aethelred's death

he lay fretting, as weak as a child, while his men fought all day against the old enemy.

The battle was over and Ethelfleda and her brother were at dinner in the manor-house of a Mercian thane when a messenger brought the news of her husband's death. Ethelfleda was silent for a long time. Then Edward spoke:

"Do not sorrow, sister. He was a good man and a brave fighter. There is still your family home in Wessex where you and your child can live in peace."

"My home is here in Mercia," replied Ethelfleda. "I am Alfred's daughter and the Lady of the Mercians will not leave her people in their time of need."

"So be it," answered Edward. "You have only to send and I will be at your side. Let us keep the bond between Mercia and Wessex and, since you have no son, let my own son Athelstan remain at your Court. He will serve you well and your stiff-necked Mercians

79

will know that there is friendship between our houses."

Ethelfleda clapped her hands. She loved her nephew who, at seventeen, was already following in the steps of his valiant grandfather. Had not Alfred girded him with his own sword when the little boy could hardly lift it? And had he not fought with that same blade in the battle that had just ended?

So, for eight years, Ethelfleda led the Mercians in peace and war and at her side was Athelstan, heir to the throne of Wessex. They rode together, the tall woman in the blue cloak and the fair-haired young warrior. Together, they fought the Danes in a new way. It was the way that a clever woman would choose.

Instead of sudden raids against the enemy and pitched battles, Ethelfleda moved steadily forward. She had forts built, called burghs or boroughs, as Alfred had done, so that if her army was forced back, there was always a stronghold in the rear.

The Danes pressed hard and they found support from the tribesmen of Wales who came down from the hills to attack a kingdom ruled by a woman. But Ethelfleda routed the Welsh and chased them into the forests. Then she ordered an advance and her men stormed the Welsh stronghold at Brecknock and captured the King of Gwent's wife and all her household.

Athelstan and Ethelfleda lead the Mercians against the Danes

Leaving troops in forts that she built along the Welsh border, the Lady of the Mercians now turned on the foe in the east.

The Danes of the Five Boroughs had long kept all the land in fear. Each town was ruled by a jarl, who had his own band of followers, but Ethelfleda defeated them one by one. In 917, she laid siege to Derby and took it by storm, while her brother Edward crushed the king of East Anglia and slew him with his jarls by the river near Huntingdon.

Next year, Leicester surrendered and the Danes of York came to ask for peace. The bearded jarls knelt and swore to obey the commands of the Lady of the Mercians. Then Ethelfleda rose and said:

"I desire only peace in this ravaged land. Let there be an end to the war between your people and mine. You shall keep the lands you have settled and the customs of your forefathers. In return, you shall take as your lord and protector, not myself, lest you chafe at a woman's rule, but my brother, Edward of Wessex."

Suddenly, she grew tired. She had ridden with her armies for eight years, had planned and schemed with her nephew and her brother, had rebuilt the churches and the people's homes and now there was peace. With her nephew, she rode back towards Mercia, but she grew weaker and the men who loved her carried her in a litter to the fort of Tamworth on Watling Street.

Here she commanded them to set in her bower the high-backed seat that was carried on all her journeys.

She was sitting there when Athelstan came in, as usual, to talk over the day's events and the orders for the morrow:

"Nephew," she said, "I have little time. With your help, the Lady of the Mercians has finished her task. When I am gone, you must not take my place. No, not yet. Your father shall rule both kingdoms as one and then, in the fullness of time, you shall be king. We have beaten the Danes, you and I, and now it is your task to make them one people with the English. One day, you shall be king, not of Wessex and Mercia, but of England."

Edmund Ironside

AS the Lady of the Mercians had foretold, Athelstan carried the banner of Wessex far into the North, defeated all the Danes and made himself King of England. After him came Edgar, another of Alfred's line, and the country was at peace.

Churches and monasteries were built. The fields were ploughed, the harvests were gathered and travellers could make their way safely along the hills.

But there was peace only when the King was strong. Edgar was followed by a weak and cowardly son, so foolish that men called him Ethelred the Unready.

When they heard that England was helpless under a feeble king and jealous earls, the Danes fitted out their dragon-ships and came raiding again. Among the sea-robbers was Sweyn Forkbeard, the warrior King of Denmark.

Ethelred had no army to fight the pirate-bands, but he said:

"I will give you ten thousand pounds in gold if you will go away."

The Danes took the gold, laughing at his simple mind. Soon they came back for more and the English people groaned when they paid the Danegeld, the tax to buy off the robbers who came and came again.

At last, Ethelred thought of a plan. There were many Danes who had settled in England, most of them peaceful folk by now, though some gave help to their kinsmen when they came raiding. Ethelred made up his mind to kill them all.

Secret orders were sent to every town. On Saint Brice's Day, 13th November 1002, all the Danes, men, women and children, were to be put to the sword. This terrible deed was carried out and, among the slaughtered, was Gunhilda, sister of Sweyn Forkbeard.

News of the massacre was carried to Denmark, where Forkbeard swore a great oath of revenge for his sister's death.

For ten years, the Danish king attacked England, landing his warriors where he pleased and thrusting inland to burn towns as far apart as Norwich, Exeter, Canterbury and Northampton. The leaderless people were in despair, for their king and the Witan did nothing to protect them, they only asked for gold.

In the year 1013, Sweyn Forkbeard and his eighteen-year-old son, Canute, landed an army in Yorkshire and made it clear that they had come to conquer the land. Sick of pillage and death, the people agreed to have Sweyn for their king. Ethelred the Unready fled to Normandy.

But Sweyn was never crowned. He died suddenly in London and young Canute went back to Denmark to ask the advice of his older brother.

Sweyn Forkbeard lands with his son, Canute

Edmund was acclaimed by the Londoners

At once, Ethelred returned, full of promises to rule well and he brought with him his son Edmund, now a young man of giant strength, as brave as his father was cowardly.

Ethelred's closest friend was a Mercian noble called Edric who was so greedy that he was known as "the Grasper". These two now set about punishing the English who had made friends with the Danes. They put some to death and took their money and land. But Edmund tried to rally his countrymen to meet the invaders.

When Canute landed, Edmund naturally expected that Edric would bring his Mercian troops to help him, but the Grasper was jealous of the young prince and he marched away to join Canute.

Wessex, Mercia and all the North were lost and

Edmund had to fall back towards London, where his father's worthless life came to an end. The stout-hearted Londoners chose Edmund for their king, but he could not stay in the city:

"Like Alfred, my forefather, I will go to the West and raise an army," he told them. "Close your gates, man the walls and keep your courage high, for I will come back to you."

While Canute brought his fleet to besiege London, Edmund raised his standard in Somerset where the Men of Wessex flocked to join him. As in Alfred's day, they hurled back the Danes, for their courage returned when they saw their young King in the thick of the fight, swinging his axe and roaring:

"On, Wessex! On! On!"

That night, as they ate and rested by the camp-fires, a harper sang of the day's victory and of their King, calling him a true leader, a man of iron.

"That's right," they shouted. "An iron king at last. Edmund Ironside, that's his name!"

The Danes retreated. At midsummer, they came on again and met Edmund's army in Wiltshire. The battle went on all day and, at nightfall, the exhausted foemen drew apart. Next day, the fight was renewed as bitterly as ever and the English seemed to be slowly pressing the enemy back when Edric the Grasper, fighting with the Danes, thought of a trick to dismay the English. Hacking off the head of a fallen man, he held it up crying:

"See the head of your King! Fly, Edmund is dead!"

Unable to reach the traitor, Edmund forced his way to a mound where he tore off his helmet to show his face:

"I live!" he cried. "Your King is here!"

He hurled a spear at Edric who escaped from the field as the furious English broke the Danish ranks.

Canute fell back and Edmund Ironside was able to relieve the brave Londoners. Then he drove some of the Danes to their ships, defeated an army in Kent and followed the rest of the Danes across the Thames into Essex.

By this time, Edric the Grasper had changed sides. He came to Edmund's tent and said:

"I ask pardon for my faults and I own you as my royal lord. The army of Mercia will fight gladly at the side of Wessex."

Edmund hated a traitor, but there were others who had joined the Danes when the English had no leader. Perhaps Edric was truly sorry. The Mercian soldiers were needed, for one more victory would drive Canute into the sea. So he took Edric's hand and placed him on the right wing of his army.

At Ashingdon in Essex, the English and the Danes faced each other from two low hills with a marshy plain between. Both armies could see the river where the Danish ships were moored side by side in their hundreds. For a time, neither side moved. Then

Edric and his troops flee from the battle

Canute, seeing the Mercians take up their position, knew that he was outnumbered. He told his men to retreat across the plain to the ships.

Edmund gave the order to charge but, as the English swept down the slope, Edric's troops stood still. At a word from their lord, they turned and marched away. Canute was too good a soldier to miss his chance. He poured his troops against the deserted flank of the English army and turned defeat into victory.

Once more, Edmund made for the West. He was not beaten, for the name of Ironside rang through the shires and he raised yet another army in Gloucestershire.

Again, he faced Canute, waiting on a hillside to open the fight when daylight came.

A horn sounded; a shout was answered and guards

brought a messenger to where Edmund was sitting with his earls. The man had come from the Danish camp:

"I bring greetings from Canute to Edmund," he said. "My lord would meet him, to speak frankly as one king to another. Canute offers peace though he stands ready for war."

The messenger was taken away and Edmund roared with laughter:

"I never thought to hear a Dane speak of peace. The cold air must have numbed his courage. To-morrow, we will cut him to pieces."

But the earls shook their heads. The land cried out for peace, they said, and this Canute was a different man from his father. He fought with honour and it would be wise to listen to what he had to say.

Edmund could not fight alone, so he went to meet Canute, unarmed, on an island in the River Severn. Each admired the other's courage and they agreed to share the kingdom. Canute should have Mercia and the Danelaw, Edmund should keep the old kingdom of Wessex. Whoever lived longest should be king over the entire country and should rule Danes and English as equals.

"It is better this way," said Canute, "two kings at peace instead of two countries at war. I would that you had been my brother, for we are too well matched to slay each other."

Edmund and Canute meet and agree to share the kingdom

Edmund looked at the Dane. "You have been a worthy foe," he answered. "Let us now live as brothers."

So England was divided once again. Canute ruled in the north and the east, and Edmund in the south, and there was peace.

But, within a year, Edmund was dead. No one knew how he died. Some said it was a sickness, but others whispered that Edric had killed him by poison to win favour from Canute.

The Dane became king over all England, swearing to rule by the laws of Alfred and Edgar. He promised to give justice to Dane and Englishman alike and he kept faith with Edmund Ironside, for he ruled wisely and he did not forget to reward Edric the Grasper with the fate that he so richly deserved.

More about the people in this book

PYTHEAS lived at Massilia (Marseilles), a Greek colony in the South of France. In about 310 B.C. he sailed to the Tin Islands and saw tin being taken at low tide to St. Michael's Mount, a trading centre off the coast of Cornwall. He went ashore in southern England and afterwards sailed far to the north. Trade in tin had been going on with the Carthaginians and with merchants from Gaul for many years, but Pytheas was the first visitor to Britain whose name is known to us.

JULIUS CAESAR (102–44 B.C.) was a gay and clever young man. His rich friend Crassus helped him to become popular with the common people of Rome through the circuses and splendid entertainments that he gave them. In 59 B.C. Caesar became Consul and Proconsul of Gaul. When he went there, no one imagined that he would become one of the greatest generals in history, for he had had little experience of warfare. His brilliant success added a huge province to the Empire, though his expeditions to Britain in 55 and 54 B.C. were carried out chiefly to punish the islanders and to impress them with the power of Rome.

Caesar's rival was Pompey, whom he defeated in a civil war through victories in Spain, Greece and Syria. The Romans made Caesar consul for life but he had only commenced to rule as absolute master of the Roman Empire when he was murdered in the Senate House in 44 B.C.

HADRIAN (A.D. 76–138) travelled widely as a young man and fought in the Roman Army against the Parthians. He succeeded his uncle Trajan as Emperor in 117 and continued his journeys until he knew more about the Empire than any other Roman.

He believed that the Empire was large enough and his aim was to establish peace, law and order behind such strong frontier defences as the famous Wall that he ordered to be built in Britain. Besides being a great builder of palaces, temples and libraries, Hadrian was a poet, musician and writer, but his character puzzled the people of his time. The lover of beauty and learning who was generous and just could also be sullen and monstrously cruel.

ETHELBURGA was the daughter of King Ethelbert and Queen Bertha of Kent to whose kingdom St. Augustine brought his band of missionaries in 597. Ethelburga married Edwin of Northumbria whom she converted to Christianity with the aid of her chaplain Paulinus, an Italian monk who had earlier joined St. Augustine's mission. When King Edwin was slain in 633, Ethelburga and Paulinus fled back to Kent where they founded a minster or "double house" for monks and nuns at Lyminge, near Folkestone. Ethelburga died there in about 647 and was later made a saint. St. Paulinus became Bishop of Rochester.

SAINT CUTHBERT lived from about 635 to 687. Little more is known about his life than is told in the story in this book. According to an unknown monk and to Bede, he was a Northumbrian shepherd-lad who entered the monastery at Old Melrose, served as a monk at Ripon and later went to Lindisfarne as prior under Abbot Eata.

Cuthbert preferred the stern life of a hermit on Farne Island but, in 684, King Ecgfrith of Northumbria, Archbishop Theodore and Trumwin, Bishop of the Picts, persuaded him to become Bishop of Lindisfarne. The strange wanderings of his coffin took place two centuries after his death. Eventually, his bones found a resting-place at Chester-le-Street and finally at Durham.

Saint Cuthbert was looked upon as the patron saint of Northumbria and his shrine was visited and enriched by any ruler who wished to win the hearts of the northerners. King Athelstan came there in 934, King Edmund in 945 and King Canute in 1020.

BEDE (A.D. 673–735) says in his *Ecclesiastical History of Britain* that he was born near the joint-monastery of Wearmouth and Jarrow and that, at the age of seven, he was taken by his relatives to be educated by Bishop Benedict and later by Abbot Ceolfrith. He continues, "I dwelt all my life from then onward in the same monastery and I gave all my labour to meditating on the scriptures. . . . I ever held it sweet to learn or to teach or to write."

Bede's list of writings included books about the Old Testament, the Temple in Jerusalem, the Prophets, and Lives of Saints as well as books on grammar, rhetoric and astronomy. In fact, he covered the whole field of knowledge in his time, but his fame rests upon his History of Britain from early times up until his own day.

ALCUIN OF YORK (A.D. 735–804), the most famous scholar in Europe, was much more a man of the world than Bede. He was, above all, a teacher and a trainer of teachers. A number of his letters still exist, including some to his friend Arno of Salzburg and to the Emperor Charlemagne.

For many years, Alcuin was chief adviser and Minister of Education to Charlemagne. Although Charlemagne's Empire fell to pieces after his death, the work of Alcuin did not perish, for he and the Emperor "had sowed the seeds of learning in Frankland" and the influence of their schools lasted for centuries.

ETHELFLEDA was the eldest child of Alfred the Great. At sixteen, she married Earl Aethelred of Gloucester, ealdorman of Mercia, and this alliance between Wessex and Mercia saved England when a huge force of Danes, led by Hasting, came over from Boulogne in 892 and made a prolonged effort to settle in that part of Mercia that lay outside the Danelaw.

After her husband's death in 912, Ethelfleda drove the Danes from Ireland back into North Wales, fortified Chester and Warwick and joined her brother, Edward the Elder, in a campaign to push back the Danes in the east and the north-east. Their success paved the way for Athelstan's later victories.

Ethelfleda must have been a remarkable woman. She accompanied her armies on campaign and won the affectionate respect of such doughty warriors as the men of Wessex and Mercia. Moreover, when she died, the Danish jarls who had surrendered to her were not prepared to obey Edward until he had proved himself as worthy a foe as his sister. She died at Tamworth in 919 and was buried at St. Peter's, Gloucester.

EDMUND IRONSIDE (A.D. 980–1016) was the son of Ethelred the Unready. After Alfred, the English Kings were Edward the Elder, Athelstan, Edmund I, "the Deed-doer", Edred, Edwy, Edgar the Peaceful and Edward the Martyr, who was murdered on the orders of his stepmother to gain the throne for her son, Ethelred the Unready.

The story in this book outlines the disastrous reign of Ethelred and the events that led to Canute's mastery of the kingdom. Canute reigned until 1035. His two unworthy sons ruled briefly and Edward the Confessor was brought from Normandy in 1042. He was the son of Ethelred and Emma of Normandy and his reign lasted until 1066.